I0054106

BITCOIN COMPLETE GUIDE FOR BEGINNERS

LEARN THE BASICS ABOUT CRYPTOCURRENCY AND HOW TO START TO MAKE PROFITS AND SUCCEED INVESTING WITH THE RIGHT MINDSET

RICHARD GLEN

COPYRIGHT

© Copyright 2021 by Richard Glen

All rights reserved.

This document is geared towards providing exact and reliable information concerning the topic and issue covered. The publication is sold with the idea that the publisher is not required to render accounting, officially permitted or otherwise qualified services. If advice is necessary, legal or professional, a practiced individual in the profession should be ordered.

- From a Declaration of Principles which was accepted and approved equally by a Committee of the American Bar Association and a Committee of Publishers and Associations.

In no way is it legal to reproduce, duplicate, or transmit any part of this document in either electronic means or printed format. Recording of this publication is strictly prohibited, and any storage of this document is not allowed unless with written permission from the publisher. All rights reserved.

The information provided herein is stated to be truthful and consistent, in that any liability, in terms of inattention or otherwise, by any usage or abuse of any policies, processes, or directions contained within is the solitary and utter responsibility of the recipient reader. Under no circumstances will any legal responsibility or blame be held against the publisher for any reparation, damages, or monetary loss due to the information herein, either directly or indirectly.

Respective authors own all copyrights not held by the publisher.

The information herein is offered for informational purposes solely and is universal as so. The presentation of the information is without a contract or any guarantee assurance.

The trademarks that are used are without any consent, and the publication of the trademark is without permission or backing by the trademark owner. All trademarks and brands within this book are for clarifying purposes only and are owned by the owners themselves, not affiliated with this document.

CONTENTS

INTRODUCTION

Bitcoin was the brainchild of Satoshi Nakamoto. Instead of designing an entirely new way to make payments and wipe out the way things can be paid for online, Satoshi looked for ways to handle existing problems within the current payment systems.

During the 2008 financial crisis, many individuals worldwide were affected by its impact on the economy. Today many people still suffer the ripple effects of that crisis on the value of their fiat currency. By the way, "fiat" refers to the government-approved official form of currency for a nation.

While the global financial system was on the verge of collapse, many central banks chose to attempt to ease the crisis by printing more money, a practice known as quantitative easing.

Quantitative Easing

As the central banks pumped money into the market to create liquidity, they also greatly reduced interest rates, intending to prevent a situation similar to the Great Depression of the 1930s. Their actions generated huge fluctuations in the country's currency values. It set off a flurry of currency wars, where nations raced to devalue their money and so make their economies stronger and more competitive than other countries.

The international response tends to be the same whenever this happens. Governments bail out their banks by printing additional money, ultimately devaluing the existing supply.

By helping the banks stay afloat, they bailed out some of the institutions whose reckless behavior had caused the crisis in the first place. The banks, who were apparently acting independently of their governments, guided many countries into unknown waters, without apparent concern that they were devaluing the nation's currency in the process.

The other choice was to let the country's economy collapse, putting it in the same situation as Iceland. When Iceland was unable to pay its debts, it experienced enormous economic instability.

A Third Option

Bitcoin offers a fresh way to think about money. It is easy to appreciate why some people are looking for creative new ways to establish a more stable economy. Because Bitcoin is transparent and decentralized, it offers an attractive alternative.

Welcome to the creation of Bitcoin, a financial organization with no connection to the few elite global decision makers. Satoshi Nakamoto decided the time was right for a different type of monetary system, a system that was different from anything currently in existence.

We don't know if Bitcoin was initially intended as a replacement for the current financial systems. However, we do know that many financial institutions are currently researching Bitcoin's technology with an eye to potentially adopting something similar for their own use. Of course, they are free to do this. The basis for Bitcoin technology, the blockchain code, has been open sourced from the beginning. Anyone can make improvements, even building whole new platforms based upon this code.

This innovation is about far more than using digital currency to pay for goods. Along with Bitcoin, the world-shaping development of blockchain technology has yet to be fully tapped.

There are many arguments about the flaws in the mainstream financial sector and any alternative is always to be welcomed. Whether Bitcoin will emerge as the alternative of choice is yet to be seen, but as the very first cryptocurrency to come out, it has great brand awareness around the world, which is a huge advantage.

Be sure to keep in mind that decentralization plays a significant role in Bitcoin. Bitcoin relies on no one: no bank, no government and no middleman. It was formed as a true peer-to-peer network in which each user doubles as part owner.

If there were no individual users, there would be no Bitcoin. The more people who embrace Bitcoin technology, the better it will work. Bitcoin depends on an ever-increasing community of people who are actively using the currency. Whether they use bitcoin to pay for goods or services, or they offer their products or services in exchange for bitcoin, active use is critical.

Digital currencies are a free market; therefore, anyone has the capability of setting up their own business anywhere across the globe and accepting bitcoin as legal tender. Processing a transaction takes a matter of minutes. Existing companies can add bitcoin as an additional method of payment, allowing them to grow swiftly from a local business to a national firm and then to expand rapidly across the worldwide market.

What's So Cool About Bitcoin?

It's almost an understatement to say the technology that powers Bitcoin is phenomenal. Bitcoin's blockchain technology is a completely new way of processing information. It is also a powerful and vital tool within the financial sector. This is not surprising, as most of Bitcoin's focus revolves around currency.

The technology behind Bitcoin provides users with options like never before. A massive amount of potential remains hidden and the best minds in the world are working to discover exactly what it will mean to see the Bitcoin technology integrated into daily life.

There is no question that the technology behind Bitcoin is seriously underestimated; however, it does have a slightly checkered past. Many platforms have been built with the sole aim of making it easier for people to use bitcoin. Unfortunately, this has not always ended well, especially in the realm of security. This type of technology involves extensive learning to understand it clearly.

The truth remains that Bitcoin is still maturing. It's young and experiencing growing pains, but we've only scratched the surface of its marvelous potential. The raw capacity behind this technology has caught the attention of a multitude of interested parties, with the forerunners coming from the financial sector.

There is much curiosity regarding the open ledger aspect of Bitcoin. Open ledger means the whole network can be viewed anytime by any individual from any location in the world. Anyone can watch transactions as they take place. While this idea may appear frightening, there are massive benefits to using a ledger that allows us to trace multiple events. None of the implementations need to be financial in nature, but a multitude of items in the financial sector are worth exploring.

There is still a lot to be investigated before you settle upon Bitcoin as a definitive method of sending and receiving payments. The decision to accept bitcoin payments on your virtual store will take only a few moments, but there are multiple implications when it comes to brick-and-mortar stores. You'll find many processors will happily assist you in exchanging between bitcoin and your local currency. The main advantages are that the processing takes a lot less time and it costs a lot less than working with credit cards or PayPal!

Bitcoin's Value

Whenever people talk about Bitcoin, the first thing they bring up is the price. Currently, the rate hovers around $6000 per bitcoin. Until 2011, bitcoin had very little value and when it began to increase in price, it was a slow process. In 2013, the bitcoin value peaked at just above $1,100; however, many believe this was because of manipulation of the biggest Bitcoin exchange at the time.

The bitcoin rate is determined by its usage and by the concept of supply and demand. Although the bitcoin supply has been limited to 21 million, experts predict this will run out by the year 2040. Nobody knows why Bitcoin has been capped at 21 million, although some believe it is related the mathematical equations involved in generating bitcoin.

We have yet to see how the bitcoin value will behave when it is more commonly used. Even though Bitcoin has been well publicized, it is still a relatively unknown quantity. We expect it to emerge from obscurity, however, as the product matures.

Worldwide financial experts view Bitcoin as a pure form of digital currency. As we get our heads around this new technology, who can say whether this term is correct? We can conclude that Bitcoin is a valid way for people to pay for purchases and this makes the digital aspect increasingly appealing. There is yet more to explore and learn, about the potential uses of Bitcoin technology.

Bitcoin gives everyone - anywhere they are in the world - the opportunity to accept a common digital currency as a form of payment. Bitcoin remains the same everywhere, so it can be converted to any form of local currency upon request. There is no transaction fee and payments

Mobile payments are increasing at a rapid rate. This adds another reason for choosing Bitcoin. It is an excellent source for mobile payments, giving businesses the ability to expand beyond national borders, at a minimal cost. Bitcoin is also an excellent investment tool if you're looking to trade in digital currency. More about this later.

Customers Drive Acceptance

Bitcoin needs to be used a lot more frequently for it to be recognized as a bona fide form of currency. Many sellers have yet to embrace Bitcoin and few buyers even know about it. As a result, it often falls on the shoulders of the Bitcoin user, to convince the other party of its merits.

The advantages for sellers are apparent: Bitcoin allows them to save on fees and other costs associated with payments. But this is only of value if customers use bitcoin to make payments. It really is up to the customers to make Bitcoin their preferred method of payment.

To make Bitcoin more convenient for buyers, a seller can offer the more familiar plastic in the form of pre-paid bitcoin cards or debit bitcoin cards. Both cards can have bitcoin deposited onto them. They can also be linked to a Bitcoin wallet, allowing the consumer to buy and sell bitcoin wherever they are accepted. Merchants pay the usual fees and receive payment in their own local currency.

While Bitcoin is far from being classified as a popular mainstream method of payment, I feel that now is the right time for people to begin using it as their go-to form of payment, even if only for the security of leaving cash and bank cards at home. Because fraud remains a constant danger, the ability to make mobile phone payments using bitcoin is increasingly viewed as a more secure option.

Widespread acceptance of bitcoin is not going to happen overnight. Until it does, those who are already using Bitcoin will need to be patient. It's good enough, for now, to know that you are already ahead of the financial curve.

CRYPTOCURRENCY AND BITCOIN

In a matter of only a few years, bitcoin has transformed from a theory into one of the era's most closely watched and intriguing investment trends. Potential for the coin and other cryptocurrencies now run the gamut, depending on whom you talk to. Some prognosticators have argued that the price of bitcoin will reach beyond $100,000. Many others claim it's a bubble on the level of the largest market mirages in history. Such is the world of cryptocurrency investing where the truth likely lies somewhere in the middle. Now that you're thinking of entering the space, make sure to embrace some of that excitement, but also keep in mind what you're buying when you declare yourself a crypto investor. It's far more than purchasing a digital coin. Here is an initial explanation of cryptocurrencies and will serve as a first step on your new journey.

What Are Cryptocurrencies?

At its basic level, cryptocurrencies are a very simple concept. They're digital coins, created online, and meant for online spending. Developed via software code, cryptos are a way to transfer value, most often via digital means, like when you're purchasing something online.

While the spending of bitcoins launched on the Internet has primarily been relegated to the online world, there are ways in which you can use them in your everyday shopping. The payment processor company Square gives its merchants the option to accept bitcoins. This allows any shop that uses Square's functionality, from the antique store to your local coffee shop, to accept bitcoins.

Take a very simple scenario, such as using a quarter to purchase a piece of gum. When you buy that gum, you're giving the quarter to a shopkeeper in order to pay for the slice of gum. The quarter is a tangible coin that a US shopkeeper trusts. He knows that if he takes the quarter, it will cover the cost of the gum and the profit that he expected to gain from the sale. It's a very predictable transaction. A quarter's value doesn't change all that dramatically in a short time. What will cost twenty-five cents today will likely run twenty-five cents tomorrow. (Over many years, that quarter won't buy you as much, due to inflation, but for the short term, it does, which is valuable for commerce.)

One bitcoin is essentially the same as a quarter except it's not tangible. It's a piece of code, and only you, as the owner, have the identifier, which is known as the coin's key. You can pass that identifier on to someone else, in order to purchase an item. That person then receives a new identifier for the bitcoin, and the old identifier becomes obsolete. You can't actually hold bitcoin. You can't feel it. But when someone accepts bitcoin, she is viewing it the same way as that quarter.

But one bitcoin has grown to become much more expensive than one slice of gum. That's because a whole community has grown around the cryptocurrency craze, willing to give bitcoin owners more and more for that one coin.

Why Would Anyone Want This Digital Coin?

If bitcoin and other cryptocurrencies function just like regular money, then why would anyone want to use them instead of the fiat currency (that is, the regular currency) that we all are used to? It's a fair question, one that the world has only begun to sort out. The answer depends greatly on who you are and why you're choosing to use the coin.

The Anti-Federal Reserve Crowd

Early adopters saw bitcoin as a tool to spend without requiring a central bank to dictate the terms of the currency. Regular currency, like the US dollar, is subject to inflation. This is, to an extent, controlled by the Federal Reserve. It increases or decreases the amount of money flowing through the world markets through its use of interest rates. On a very basic level, when there's more money flowing into the market, then the supply rises, decreasing the value of one dollar. When the Fed restricts dollars, then the value rises. The Federal Reserve does this to retain a consistent inflation rate, so the economy doesn't grow too fast. Hyper-growth can lead to an overvaluation of goods you purchase, which would hurt the currency. Hyperinflation leads to a devaluation of the currency altogether and the Federal Reserve is mandated to try and hold inflation in check.

This is a very simplistic definition of inflation. Since the economy has become global in nature, there are a lot of factors that would increase demand in the US dollar, like a devaluation of a foreign currency. The Federal Reserve must account for all of those factors, as it sets interest rates.

Digital coin enthusiasts don't believe that government entities should have the power to dictate these fluctuations in the money supply. One of the original goals of a cryptocurrency is to avoid inflation altogether. That's why bitcoin has a maximum number of coins—21 million—it can ever have in circulation.

The Business Case for Cryptocurrencies

What started as a libertarian dream, however, actually has a legitimate business use. It costs money to spend money. As odd as that is, there's a reason banks and financial institutions have grown so large. It's because they can collect fees in countless number of ways as money moves through their systems. For businesses, this can become very costly.

One of the easiest ways to imagine this is when you're going on a trip to Europe and you have to exchange dollars for euros. When you go to the exchange counter at the airport, you not only receive less money back than you put in—because the dollar is worth less than a euro—but you also lose a large chunk to a fee that the exchange agency charges to give you the euro. Now imagine that on a wide scale, where a business is making exchanges in the millions of dollars every day. Clearly there is an incentive to reduce that cost.

The US Treasury handles the actual dollar development and distribution, but it's dictated by the interest rate determined by the Federal Reserve. If the Fed decreases the interest rate, then it encourages banks to borrow more funds since the cost has dropped. Rate increases discourage borrowing, since it's expensive, and therefore, less money flows through the financial system.

That's where a digital coin has an advantage, since it isn't tangible. It can serve as an independent third party. Instead of going to a teller, you could use bitcoin to exchange the dollars by buying bitcoin with US dollars then selling them for euros once in Europe. The transaction is processed on bitcoin's decentralized platform, leaving the transaction fee for processing the digital coin as the only fee the company has to pay. That saves you the cost of the much higher exchange fee created by the middleman. Financial institutions and other organizations are seeing the value of that, particularly in areas where the local currencies aren't as stable.

The Everyday Use of Cryptocurrencies

When evaluating why you and other regular spenders of currency would want to use cryptocurrencies, the conversation becomes a little more difficult. While there are benefits to a digital coin that's un-hackable, lives online, and will transfer almost immediately to the retailer when you purchase an item, it hasn't outweighed the ease of use and trust in the American dollar. Whether cryptos become a more prominent tool for everyday purchases depends on the ease of use. Regular consumers are going to spend the currency that's safest and simplest for them to use. Right now, that's the US dollar. If there was a reason for bitcoin or another cryptocurrency to replace the US dollar, and it was as easy to use as dollars are today, then it could grow. But that reality hasn't presented itself yet.

It's, however, still early days in cryptocurrency usage. To get a sense of just how early, let's look at how the entire market began.

An Origin Story

Maybe you believe you already know how you feel about cryptocur-rencies. Maybe you're reading this to get an understanding of what exactly cryptocurrencies are before rushing to judgment. Either way, you should know where they come from in order to theorize about their future. Their origin story also provides a backdrop on why the technology supporting cryptocurrencies has the potential to shift the way the world operates.

Satoshi Nakamoto and the Creation of Bitcoin

Bitcoin, the original cryptocurrency, has an origin story that contains a number of mysteries, mostly because the creator of the coin has never come forward and proven that he or she published the concepts that would launch the crypto craze and form what you now known as bitcoin.

In 2008, an author using the pseudonym Satoshi Nakamoto published a paper outlining a new structure to develop a decentralized, peer-to-peer currency. In the paper, Nakamoto explains the concept of the blockchain, which produces a decentralized digital ledger and will become the backbone to bitcoin. Many enthusiasts had attempted to launch a digital currency in the early 2000s, but it wasn't until this framework published—in which the notion of the blockchain was described—that the ability to structure a currency completely decentralized from any oversight was shown to be possible. The author of the paper remains a mystery to this day.

Nakamoto's vision worked because she or he conceptualized the notion of removing the requirement of trust in order to process a payment. For instance, when you pay by check, you're trusting that the bank will provide the funds to the vendor based on what's in your checking account. The vendor accepts the check, trusting that the bank will ensure you have the funds for the service provided. The concept Nakamoto described removed the notion that vendors and consumers needed a third party, such as a bank, to provide this trust. Instead, this blockchain, or digital ledger, would verify the information as the transaction unfolds. Therefore, if you were trying to spend all your bitcoins on a car, the blockchain would first double check all the transactions ever provided by you to ensure you have the funds to supply the car dealer with the number of bitcoins required for the purchase. Trust is no longer a factor—the blockchain verifies that you have the funds. This opens up dramatic opportunities to bypass traditional financial systems.

To this day, despite many efforts to uncover the person or group behind the pseudonym, the identity of Nakamoto remains a mystery. Some have claimed that Craig Wright, an Australian entrepreneur, is Nakamoto. But efforts by Wright to prove this have fallen short.

Nakamoto has an estimated 980,000 bitcoins, based on analyses done in the early days of bitcoin's popularity. If this number holds true, then when bitcoin's price rises, Nakamoto's crypto wealth matches some of the richest people in the world. At bitcoin's peak, Nakamoto's paper wealth placed him just behind Paul Allen, the cofounder of Microsoft, on the Forbes 400: The Wealthiest in America list.

Bitcoin Changes Everything

Shortly after this concept paper was published, Nakamoto created the first bitcoin. This technological breakthrough—the blockchain—separated bitcoin from all other prior attempts to develop online or digital currency. From this code and concept, many other cryptocurrencies have been birthed in an effort to fix problems within bitcoin, improve upon what Nakamoto started, or to jump into the cryptocurrency craze in search of a quick buck.

METHODS TO GET BITCOIN

Once you have somewhere to put your funds, you can actually get some Bitcoin! There are a number of ways that someone can get Bitcoin, but the most common are:

- By exchanging fiat currency for Bitcoin through an exchange
- Getting Bitcoin from someone else who already has Bitcoin
- Bitcoin mining

We will look at all of these methods, but before we dive in, we should step back and look at a more fundamental question: Where do Bitcoins come from?

Where Do Bitcoins Come From?

Who "makes" bitcoins? This is an important question, and it is relating to another issue that you may be wondering about: how is the value of bitcoin determined?

To answer both of these questions, it is helpful to look briefly at where traditional fiat currency comes from. Broadly speaking, governments and institutions control the printing of paper money. The amount of money that is printed impacts the value of that currency in the global financial market. The economics behind how this all works can get pretty complicated, but in a nutshell: the more money a government prints, the less value that currency generally has. In economic terms, this principal is often referred to as "scarcity," meaning that the less there is of something and the more people that want it, the more value that thing has. This concept applies to commodities, fiat currencies, and Bitcoin.

There are many examples throughout history of situations where a government has printed tons of paper money to cover short-term expenses (almost always related to war), and as a result the value of that currency has plummeted. Probably the most well-known example of this is the hyperinflation that occurred in Germany's Weimer Republic after World War I. People famously wallpapered their houses with paper money because it had so little value.

One significant way that Bitcoin is different than fiat currency is that there is a hard cap to the number of Bitcoins that will be created. No more than 21 million Bitcoins will ever exist. The last Bitcoin is estimated to appear sometime around the year 2140. This built-in scarcity is one crucial aspect of how the value of Bitcoin is determined.

Still, however, we have not really answered the question of where Bitcoins actually come from. The short answer is that they are "mined" by Bitcoin miners.

Bitcoin Mining

If Bitcoins come from mining, it might be quite tempting to conclude that one should drop everything and become a Bitcoin miner. One of the first things that newcomers to the Bitcoin space often hear about is mining. At a glance, this can look like a primrose path to "free money." It can sound like mining is as easy as firing up an application your laptop and watching the Bitcoins come rolling in! Unfortunately, like most things involving "free money," the reality is that mining is not so simple.

Earlier we looked at the blockchain and how transactions are stored throughout a distributed network of computers. We know that each transaction is verified and added the blockchain, but how exactly does this happen?

This is where miners come in. Bitcoin miners use special software to solve complex math problems that are used to verify transactions, maintain the blockchain and add blocks. By checking a new transaction against the public ledger of preceding transactions (the blockchain), a "node" (a particular mining station) is able to distinguish between a valid transaction and an invalid one.

If someone attempts to spend Bitcoins that don't exist the system will say, "Hey, wait a minute, this doesn't match up with the history on the blockchain..." and the transaction will be rejected. Miners handle the heavy-duty computer processing that it takes to check all new Bitcoin transactions, verify them, and add them to the blockchain.

In exchange for solving blocks, miners are rewarded with a certain amount of new Bitcoin, thus adding a little bit at a time to the global volume of available Bitcoins in circulation. This incentive encourages more people to mine, leading to a more secure system through wider distribution.

In the early days of Bitcoin, mining was something that could be done on pretty much any old computer and the reward for "discovering" a block was ample, while the overall value of Bitcoin was extremely low and there were not that many Bitcoins in circulation. Over time, as more and more people began to use Bitcoin, and also to become miners, the conditions changed.

Built in to the protocol behind Bitcoin is a relationship between the number of miners and the level of difficulty involved in solving the problem, or "mining" each block. In theory, we can imagine that if more miners enter into the scene, more blocks will be created at a faster pace. The Bitcoin protocol works in such a way that as more blocks are created, the rate of difficulty involved in solving the complex math problems required to successfully "mine" a block goes up. By making it harder to mine a block, the rate of block creation goes down. This relationship between the number of Bitcoins that exist and the level of difficulty involved in mining new ones keeps the ecosystem stable over time.

The level of difficulty, today, required to mine a block is so resource-heavy, both in computer power and electricity, that it requires special equipment. In most cases, the cost of a mining operation far outweighs what one could hope to earn from mining Bitcoin for a very long time. Many miners today operate in collectives known as "pools," where members combine resources and split rewards. Joining a mining pool is one way to increase the odds of recouping the costs of mining equipment and potentially making a profit. It is still possible to earn Bitcoin today through mining, but it is definitely not easy or free to get started.

Buying Bitcoin

While there is still opportunity in mining, it is definitely not the most straightforward way to get your hands on some Bitcoin. It is much faster and easier to get existing Bitcoin from somewhere else, rather than trying to mine new Bitcoin.

When it comes to acquiring Bitcoin in this way, you have several options. No matter which route you take, you will need to set up a Bitcoin wallet to receive and store your funds.

Bitcoin Exchanges

In many countries, the easiest way to buy Bitcoin with fiat currency is through an online exchange. Bitcoin exchanges work essentially just like any other currency exchange, where you use one currency to buy another. At the time of this writing, Coinbase is one of the most popular Bitcoin exchanges in the US. Coinbase is an online platform that creates a Bitcoin wallet for you, lets you connect your bank account, and buy or sell Bitcoin through a very simple user interface.

Most Bitcoin exchanges involve transaction fees, and Coinbase is no exception. While it is technically "free" to use most Bitcoin exchanges, there will percentage fees associated with most or all transactions. It also not uncommon to experience delays when transacting through exchanges, which can range from mildly inconvenient to debilitating. Becoming familiar with the process and factoring fees and delay times into your transactions will make things run much more smoothly.

Most exchanges that allow you to buy Bitcoin with fiat currency will require you to link to a bank account and enter some personal information. This allows for fast, convenient movement between fiat currency and Bitcoin. Once again, it will be worth it to do some research and be sure to use an exchange that can demonstrate some longevity and has a good reputation.

Even then, it is generally not a good idea to store all or most of your Bitcoin in an online exchange. Mt. Gox, famously, was the world's dominant Bitcoin exchange for several years. At the height of its popularity, Mt. Gox handled around 70% of the world's total Bitcoin transactions. Then, in 2014, there was a massive security breach and approximately 850,000 Bitcoins were lost or stolen under somewhat mysterious circumstances. Exchanges are useful for moving funds between Bitcoin and fiat, trading, and actively transacting with Bitcoin, but the Mt. Gox fiasco is a good example of why it is not the best idea to keep all of your assets stored in an online exchange.

Bitcoin ATMS

Another way to buy Bitcoin that is becoming increasingly popular is through Bitcoin ATMs. These devices are cropping up all over the place, from malls to airports to city centers. They look a lot like traditional ATM's, but there are some important differences. Primarily, Bitcoin ATMs don't connect to any banks. They are connected, through the Internet, only to the universe of the Bitcoin network. Many Bitcoin ATMs allow for bi-directional exchange, meaning that you can either insert cash to be converted to Bitcoin and transferred to a public key address, or you can have Bitcoins from your own account converted into cash and dispensed by the machine. Some only handle transfers one-way or the other.

ATM's can provide a more anonymous way to buy into Bitcoin without syncing your bank account to a platform like Coinbase. However, there may be high transaction fees and limits on how much you can deposit or withdraw depending on the machine. One way that you can search for Bitcoin ATMs in your area is by using the Coin ATM Radar website.

Getting Bitcoin from Someone Else

Since the very beginning of Bitcoin, one of the most common ways to get started the currency has been to find someone willing to gift or sell some to you. As Bitcoin is a digital asset, it should not be too surprising that much of the Bitcoin community exists online. Forums such as bitcointalk.org or Reddit's r/bitcoin are good places to engage with other Bitcoin users. Some Bitcoin enthusiasts are happy to donate a small amount to a newcomer to help them establish their first wallet. After all, the more people that use Bitcoin, the higher the demand, thus the more valuable it will become, at least in theory. Through that lens, it makes sense from a long-term financial perspective to help new users get started even if means spending a little of your own coin initially.

There are also a variety tools online to find local Bitcoin exchanges, where people actually meet up offline, in person, to trade with Bitcoin. This can be a great method to avoid transaction fees, meet fellow Bitcoin enthusiasts in your area, and potentially increase the level of transaction anonymity. As with any scenario that involves meeting someone "from the Internet," use your judgment if meeting up to exchange Bitcoin locally.

COMMON BITCOIN MYTHS

Myth: Bitcoin Uses Too Much Energy and Is Bad for The Environment

Bitcoin miners do use a lot of electricity. Clickbait articles like to compare Bitcoin miners' electricity usage to that of small countries. Of course, the same critique might be made of the Internet, which uses 10% of global electricity. You'll have to decide for yourself whether cat videos and clickbait articles about Bitcoin's energy usage are a good use of global electricity. I personally think that the internet is worth it. Higher civilizations use more energy than low civilizations. If you live in a mud hut, your energy consumption will be very low. If you are part of a globally connected space-faring civilization, your energy usage will be much, much higher. Fortunately, there are nearly infinite energy sources in the solar system. Fusion and Dyson spheres will power our global civilization to the next level.

It's also unfair to criticize Bitcoin's energy usage without examining the trade-offs. Mining gold uses huge amounts of energy, and can be quite hard on the environment. The fiat financial system also uses a lot of energy. Think of all those Brinks trucks, and ATMs, and perpetually empty bank branches, with their heating and lighting costs. Printing up new paper money and coins also uses large amounts of natural resources and energy. Then there is the financial cost of human energy that is confiscated through monetary inflation.

No one criticizes a bank or brokerage (or Fort Knox) for using a lot of energy to secure wealth. You cannot just leave gold bars out in the open— they require physical security. Bank and brokerage accounts also require digital or cryptographic security, both of which use electricity.

Bitcoin is the most secure bank in the cloud. It is secured by real work carried out by Bitcoin mining computers. The high hash rate of the Bitcoin network ensure that it is a harmless and protected place to store wealth. Bitcoin is a scarce, decentralized, seizure-resistant, and censorship-resistant way to store value. Why should something like that be free or low cost? Would you ever consider using a low-cost solution to secure a Picasso painting or the Hope Diamond?

In addition, a lot of people don't realize that a substantial amount of Bitcoin mining is powered by renewable energy (solar, wind, hydropower) or "stranded" energy sources. Stranded natural gas is often flared or vented into the atmosphere, if it is not cost-efficient to build a pipeline to move the gas. Rather than being wasted like this, there are now companies who are using this stranded natural gas to power Bitcoin mining machines.

Myth: Bitcoin Is A Bubble

There has never been a bubble that popped and then came back to new highs just a few years later. Individuals who don't have a lot of involvement with markets will often call a particular market a bubble. Observers have been calling the California housing market a bubble for the past 50 years, and yet housing prices continue to march higher almost every year. Amazon was called a bubble, but turned out to be simply one of the best businesses of all time. Just because an asset like

Apple or Amazon goes up a lot in price does not mean that it is a bubble.

Now that Bitcoin is once again hitting new all-time highs, the burden of proof is on the critics. What would they need to see for their hypothesis to be falsified? Peter Schiff has been declaring that Bitcoin is a bubble since 2013, when it was trading at $375. Why would anyone continue to listen to him?

Myth: Bitcoin Is a Ponzi Scheme or Scam

Bitcoin is completely decentralized. It is not controlled by one group, but rather control is spread across the community of miners, full nodes, developers, and Bitcoin holders. It's not like XRP, which was issued by a centralized corporation that is now being sued by the SEC. For something to be a Ponzi, you need a central ringleader like Charles Ponzi or Bernie Madoff. Most serious Bitcoiners will tell you that they will never sell their Bitcoin. This is not how pump and dump schemes generally work.

Myth: Bitcoin Is Just for Criminals

Simply not true. US regulators now allow US banks to custody Bitcoin. Anyone can buy Bitcoin using PayPal. Billionaires and blue-chip corporations are moving their cash into Bitcoin. Anyone who says that Bitcoin is just for criminals has not been following the news. Bitcoin is now a mainstream asset, which anyone can hold.

Now this does mean that there are no bad actors who use Bitcoin. Because there is no centralized authority who decides who can and who cannot use Bitcoin, anyone can use it— for good or evil. Just like anyone can use fire or a chemical compound for good or evil. That being said, the bulk of the world's illegal and illicit activities are still carried out using US dollars. Cryptographers, software developers, and other nerdy types who like Bitcoin usually lead fairly boring and law-abiding lives.

Myth: The Government Will Ban Bitcoin

The U.S. government is certainly not going to ban Bitcoin anytime soon. Bitcoin will be regulated and taxed in the U.S., but not banned. A country that bans Bitcoin is like a country that bans the internet. It will lose its best and brightest and wealthiest, who will move to a more friendly jurisdiction. As we mentioned before, you can take your Bitcoin anywhere in the world that you want, using nothing more than a "brain wallet." If the U.S. eventually bans Bitcoin, there will be a friendly country somewhere (Cayman? Singapore?) that will do everything that it can to attract those displaced Bitcoiners. What country doesn't want wealthy and educated immigrants?

The Bitcoin software is currently being run on more than 11,000 computers around the world.

A government can try to shut down all of the full nodes inside of its border, but how can it shut down the full nodes that are operating in another country? If the U.S. decides to ban Bitcoin, it can try to shut down all full nodes in the U.S. But the Bitcoin network will keep running in other countries. China and Russia might just decide that they don't want to go along with the U.S. and ban Bitcoin. A lot of other countries resent the "exorbitant privilege" conveyed by US Dollars and would like to see this system come to an end.

Even if it wanted to, the U.S. could never shut down all of the full nodes, even within its borders. How do you seize all of the computers that are running an open-source software program? Open-source software is currently protected under the First Amendment in the U.S.

If you do try to shut down people running the software, someone can just fire up a new computer, download the Bitcoin software, and get up and running again. Bitcoin is more difficult to stop than cannabis or alcohol, both of which the U.S. government tried and failed to shut down. Let's not forget the fact that billionaires and Wall Street also love Bitcoin now, and they have the lobbying power to protect it.

The billionaire Chamath Palihapitiya already owns 1 million Bitcoin. Other billionaires like the Winklevoss twins have been scooping up Bitcoin and stashing it away in cold storage. Like all good money, Bitcoin is being hoarded and taken out of circulation. This process has accelerated in 2020, with the entrance of institutional investors into the game. Famous hedge fund managers like Paul Tudor Jones and Stanley Druckenmiller have been buying Bitcoin. The billionaire Michael Saylor bought 17,732 Bitcoins for himself and another 40,824 Bitcoins for his publicly traded company (MicroStrategy).

Anyone who tells you that Bitcoin is going to be banned in the U.S. has simply not been paying attention. Good luck getting legislators to ban something that U.S. billionaires and Wall Street love. Why would regulators allow U.S. banks to custody Bitcoin (as they did in 2020), if they were planning on making Bitcoin illegal?

Myth: Bitcoin Has No Value Because Anyone Can Easily Create Their Own Cryptocurrency

Anyone can fork (copy) the Bitcoin software, but no one can fork the Bitcoin ecosystem. You can create your own cryptocurrency, but how are you going to persuade all of the full nodes, miners, developers, and investors to accept your new cryptocurrency? I can easily create my own social networking software, but it doesn't mean that I will be able to steal users from Facebook. The real value is in the network of people who interact with the software, rather than the software itself.

Myth: Bitcoin Will Be Replaced by A Competitor

Bitcoin is a money protocol. The internet still runs on old protocols like TCP/IP, HTTP, and SMTP. In a perfect world they would be better, but they stick around because they are "good enough." Bitcoin does a really good job of securing value in a trustless, uncensorable manner. Bitcoin is "good enough." Facebook supplanted MySpace because it didn't cost anything to open up an account on both networks. It's impossible to store your savings simultaneously in

Bitcoin and in a new competing cryptocurrency, without first selling off some of your Bitcoin and using it to purchase the new crypto.

Bitcoin is protected by its strong network effects. Buyers go to Amazon because that's where all of the sellers are; sellers go to Amazon because that's where all of the buyers are. Bitcoin has the largest market cap, highest security (highest hash rate), and highest liquidity of any cryptocurrency, which makes it an ideal candidate for institutional investors. This creates a virtuous circle where Bitcoin gets even larger and more secure, the more institutional investors buy it.

Bitcoin is good at doing some very basic things— storing value and making it possible to send that value anywhere in the world. If you added more bells and whistles, it would only increase the attack surface of Bitcoin. Over time, there will be additional layers built on top of Bitcoin (like the Lightning Network, for example). But the foundation will stay the same. Only Bitcoin offers this highly secure, neutral, global settlement layer.

Myth: Bitcoin Has No Intrinsic Value Because It Is Not Backed by Anything

The US dollar has also not been backed by anything, since at least 1971 when the U.S. officially left the gold standard. Nevertheless, the US dollar still functions as money. Some people think that a commodity needs to have industrial or practical use to function as money. This was certainly true of gold and sea-shells in the past (both could be used to make beautiful jewelry).

Humanity is now rapidly moving into the digital age, where we spend most of our waking hours in virtual worlds like social media and gaming. The younger generations intuitively get that Bitcoin fits in perfectly in this new digital existence. Bitcoin is easy to store and to send, and it is the best store of value available. You cannot make a necklace out of Bitcoin, but Millennials and Generation Z could care less.

Facebook also has no intrinsic value— it's just a bunch of 0's and 1's like Bitcoin. It's the network that has value— the fact that billions of people are willing to upload content and engage on the network. Bitcoin is also just a bunch of 0's and 1's, but it is "backed" (like Facebook) by the millions (and soon billions) of people who choose to interact with the network.

Anyone who says that something immaterial like software cannot be extremely valuable has clearly been asleep for the past 20 years.

METHODS OF SELLING BITCOIN

Cashing out your Bitcoins isn't as clear as getting them. In case you choose to sell your Bitcoins online, you can either do it using trade, direct exchange or complete a shared exchange.

Exchanges

Despite having a few disadvantages, exchanges are a one-stop solution with regards to exchanging Bitcoins. On account of selling the cryptographic money, trades act as an intermediary that holds both dealer's and purchaser's assets.

To start with, you need to set up an account with a trade of your decision. The outright dominant part of trustworthy trades will require verification with complete identity and an associated financial balance so you can withdraw your funds.

At that point, you place a 'sell offer,' expressing the kind of money you wish to exchange, its amount, and your asking cost per unit. The trade will consequently finish the exchange once somebody coordinates your offer.

After the assets are credited to your account, you should withdraw them to your kinked bank account. This can once in a while take an excessive amount of time, particularly if the trade is encountering issues with its banks or confronting liquidity issues. A while before its bankruptcy, the Mt. Gox trade was experiencing this careful issue. Besides, a few banks simply through and through decline to process transactions with funds acquired using cryptocurrency trading.

It is also crucial to consider a fee you'll have to pay to utilize a few exchanges. For instance, one of the world's greatest cryptocurrency exchanges, CEX.io, charges a flat fee of $50 for withdrawal using Bank move, $3.80 in case you're pulling out your assets to a Visa card in addition 1.2 percent of a deal + $3.80 in case you're utilizing MasterCard. The withdrawal charges can differ relying upon an exchange; however, exchange expenses are quite often either small or non-existent at all.

Furthermore, most exchanges will have a breaking point on the measure of cash you're allowed to store. The limit will increase over the long run if you stay loyal to a particular exchange.

At long last, it is essential to remember that despite offering wallet services, exchanges are by no means a protected and dependable place to store your assets. They are prone to hacker attacks, and there have also been cases of exchanges closing down and running away with their clients' assets. Consequently, you should assume full liability for your funds and store any amount that isn't immediately required in a protected offline wallet.

Direct Trades

Another strategy for selling your Bitcoins is through a direct exchange with someone else. This assistance is open on sites generally connected with trades and incorporates an intermediary facilitating the connection.

To begin with, you should register as a seller. Aside from setting up your profile, you should completely verify your identity. Whenever you're registered, you can post an offer showing your intention to sell some Bitcoins. When a purchaser needs to trade with you, you get a notification from the service, and from that point on, you are just interacting with the buyer. The site only serves as a platform to finish the trade.

The way toward selling Bitcoins on a portion of those sites can be very included and time-consuming. Thus, it is basic to do your research before choosing a trading platform and ensure you have the time and patience required.

A portion of the sites offering the option of direct trading is BitBargain, Bittylicious, Coinbase, Openbitcoins, Bitsquare, and LocalBitcoins.

Online P2P trading

Peer-to-peer trading commercial centers are a moderately new development in the Bitcoin world. There is no direct trade of funds that are taking place. However, those sites fill in as a platform that brings individuals with different but complementary requirements.

The help is intended for the mutual benefit of individuals who might want to purchase Bitcoins with their credit card and the individuals who need to spend their Bitcoins to purchase products from places that don't acknowledge advanced monetary standards a type of payment. Therefore, the preceding get their level cash traded to BTC, while the last can buy limited products.

The sites facilitating the service furnish clients with an escrow service for the trade, just as a wallet to store Bitcoins.

Here's the way it works:

Bob posts his necessary list of things to get, including the discount amount he wishes to get, which regularly goes up to 25 percent. Then Jack accepts the exchange and pays for Bob's goods through the market place, expressing Bob's delivery address. When the goods are delivered, the commercial center delivers Jack's cash from escrow and transfers the funds into Jack's wallet.

While this framework allows Jack to get Bitcoins relatively effectively utilizing only his bank card, it also charges him quite a high service fee.

A portion of the sites offering this support is Purse, Brawker, and OpenBazaar.

All the mentioned services above are online-based centralized stages. To have the option to sell Bitcoins utilizing those services, you will typically have to completely verify your identification, which voids Bitcoin trading its anonymity. Also, whenever you've figured out how to sell your BTCs, you should withdraw the funds into your bank account or a bank card. As a general rule, this process will take quite a while and will bring about some fees.

Consequently, many individuals are picking offline trading.

Through ATM

Despite looking at traditional cash machines, Bitcoin ATMs are not ATMs in the traditional sense. Rather than associating with the user's bank account, they are associated with the Internet to have the option to facilitate Bitcoin transactions.

Bitcoin ATMs can acknowledge money in real money and trade it to Bitcoins given a receipt of paper with a QR-code on it or by moving the resources for a wallet on a Blockchain association. They ordinarily charge high exchange expenses; media reports are alluding to charges as high as seven percent.

Also, they can be very hard to find. Most known Bitcoin ATMs are set apart on this Bitcoin ATM map.

Now and again, Bitcoin ATM suppliers require clients to have a current account to conduct selling activities, and the registration process frequently includes a lot of time, effort, and energy. For instance, new clients of Robocoin ATM need a phone number for notifications and activation, a government-provided ID, a palm check, and a current photograph taken by the ATM's webcam. The identification process varies depending upon the machine and even on various operators running similar ATMs; however, some kind of identity verification will consistently be required if you need to sell.

After your identity is checked, you are given a QR code with a wallet address to which you need to send your Bitcoins. Depending on the machine you're utilizing, you will either get cash out of the machine promptly, or you will get a recovery code and need to wait for the transaction confirmation. Generally, one confirmation is sufficient, however at times, up to six confirmations are needed before the client can withdraw cash.

Along these lines, despite the ever-growing number of Bitcoin ATMs around the world, they are still primarily used to purchase Bitcoins. Also, BTC ATM operators need to change their machines' setting as hostile to anti-money laundering and know your client standards material in the jurisdiction where their ATMs are set. In some countries, this requires a cash transmitter license, while current guidelines in different countries keep any Bitcoin ATMs from being installed.

Selling Bitcoin in Person

From various perspectives, digital trading currency in person is probably at least somewhat simple. All you need to do to retail your Bitcoins is scan a QR-code on somebody's telephone and get money on the spot. In case you're offering to friends or family members, you just need to set them up with a Bitcoin wallet, send them the fundamental sum and gather your money.

However, if you manage a random person, you will doubtlessly experience extensive rounds of negotiations examining the value, spot of meeting, and other applicable conditions. Besides, you need to take a couple of things to guarantee your security and your funds' safety.

How to Negotiate the Price?

Some various sites and forums assist traders in arranging a one-on-one gathering to purchase, furthermore, sell Bitcoin, with Local

Bitcoins being the most generally utilized stage. One of its primary favorable circumstances is the rating framework, which implies you can evaluate the reliability of individuals you wish to trade with.

As Bitcoin's worth continually fluctuates, the final exchange rate is regularly settled during the meeting. Most traders use rates from prominent exchanges. On the other hand, services like Bitcoin Price Index can be utilized. Now and then, sellers will charge a fee on top of Bitcoin's current exchange rate for comfort, anonymity, and to take care of their costs. Picking the measure of the said fee is completely up to you, but normally it is set at around five to 10 percent.

Besides, it is important to know about local fluctuations in Bitcoin's cost. The exchange rate can be diverse, relying upon a country. This is related to difficulties in getting Bitcoin with the local, national currency.

Then again, rather than setting up a one-on-one meeting in advance, you could visit your local Bitcoin get together. There are various such meet-ups worldwide, during which the participants are glad to purchase and sell Bitcoin and other digital currencies. It is likely the most secure climate to conduct person-to-person trades. When selling at a meet-up, you should be ready to negotiate the cost on the spot.

Recommendations for Remaining Safe

Offering Bitcoin person-to-person is the ideal trading option for individuals who value convenience and anonymity. In any case, security considerations, particularly when trading with a total outsider from the Internet, are of utmost significance.

Most importantly, carefully, you should pick a spot for the meeting. It must be a public place with dynamic Internet access, as both of you should have the option to get to your online wallets. Bringing a companion along to the gathering is normal person-to-person trading; however, it is crucial to advise the purchaser before the meeting.

Avoid the potential risk you would while conveying a major measure of money. Be ready, keep away from public vehicles and never meet in private homes.

Withdrawing Funds

In case you're selling Bitcoins on the web, you will face the issue of withdrawing funds. The most well-known approach to move cash is international wire move, and most prominent trades uphold this technique for transferal. As of late, nonetheless, a few trades started to accept credit and debit card withdrawals.

On the other hand, cash can be transferred via SEPA, representing the Single European Payments Area. It is a framework designed to make international transfers between individuals from the European Union more effective. Some European cryptocurrency exchanges accept this method of transferal.

However, both of these frameworks are a long way from perfect. Moves, as a rule, take an exceptionally long time, contingent upon the country and the measure of money being transferred, they can require as long as four days to be processed. Moreover, both these frameworks bring about additional charges. For instance, Barclay's bank charges £25 to £40, contingent upon how quickly you need the transfer to be done for a SEPA payment. Conversely, HSBC just charges £4 for a SEPA payment made using online banking; however, HSBC is famous for refusing to work with Bitcoin and some other digital currency-related funds.

FREQUENTLY ASKED QUESTIONS

Ever since the price of bitcoin surpassed $20,000 at the end of 2020, I've been asked numerous times by friends and family how they can buy BTC. Initially, I tried to help everyone by getting on video calls to show them how to purchase small amounts of bitcoin.

While there are a number of legally operating cryptocurrency exchanges in the United States, my go-to platform for newcomers based in the U.S. has been PayPal. On Oct. 21, 2020, PayPal announced support for cryptocurrency, noting that all eligible users in the U.S. could buy, sell and hold bitcoin, along with a few other popular cryptocurrencies, on their platform.

While impressive, I've chosen to introduce newcomers to bitcoin via PayPal mainly due to the fact that the platform is well known and generally trusted by the mainstream. This is helpful for a number of reasons, especially since most people already have a PayPal account, therefore they don't need to download a new app. Buying bitcoin on PayPal is also pretty straightforward.

For now, I think it's important to address a few common questions.

"Do I Have to Buy A Whole Bitcoin?"

The answer is no, you do not have to buy a whole bitcoin in order to own BTC. In fact, it's very common for people to buy "bits of bitcoin," also known as "Sats," which is shorthand for "satoshis." This popular crypto term – named after Satoshi Nakamoto – is used to describe the smallest possible denomination of BTC, which is one-hundred millionth of a bitcoin.

Going back to PayPal as an example, U.S. users can buy as little as $1 dollar worth of BTC per day on the platform. According to PayPal's cryptocurrency fact page, the maximum dollar amount for weekly cryptocurrency purchases is $10,000. The maximum dollar amount for purchases over a 12-month period is $50,000.

With this in mind, PayPal offers a great option for U.S. users looking to buy small amounts of BTC. However, the platform would not be ideal for those wanting to buy a whole bitcoin (at least not as of writing this book since the price of one BTC is currently fluctuating between $38,000 and $48,000 USD).

Another familiar option for buying small amounts of bitcoin would be through a bitcoin ATM. Each time I grocery shop at Safeway, I pass the Coinstar kiosk machine. The front of the machine mentions that bitcoin can be bought at the kiosk with cash (in my case USD).

According to the Coinstar website, this is how one would go about buying bitcoin at a kiosk location:

Go to a select Coinstar kiosk, touch "Buy Bitcoin," study and accept the transaction terms, and enter your phone number.

Insert U.S. paper money into the cash acceptor (any amount up to $2,500)

Receive voucher with a bitcoin redemption code.

Create an account or sign in to your existing account to claim your bitcoin at coinme.com/redeem.

Although the process is straightforward, one would still need to create an account through Coinme to claim their BTC. That being said, it's important to know that Coinme was the first state-licensed bitcoin ATM company in the United States. Coinme ATMs are now deployed across various locations worldwide. As of December 2020, the Coinme service has been made available in nearly 25% of Coinstar's total kiosk fleet with locations in 40 U.S. states.

Another question I've recently been asked is:

"What Fees Are Associated with Buying Bitcoin?"

This is a great question. Now that you know you can buy bits of bitcoin, understanding the fees is important.

Going back to PayPal as an example, the payment provider did not charge any fees to buy bitcoin before 2021. This means if you bought BTC on PayPal in December 2020, there were no fees for doing so, which is awesome.

But as of 2021 PayPal has started charging a small fee for buying or selling bitcoin. Like most cryptocurrency exchanges, there is no fee for holding bitcoin in your PayPal account.

There is also a fee when buying bitcoin at a Coinstar kiosk. According to a recent Yahoo Finance article, there is a 4% fee to purchase Bitcoin with cash, along with a spread.

Fees and spreads for buying and selling bitcoin are very common. According to Investopedia, cryptocurrency exchanges typically add fees when users purchase and sell coins. This means you will be charged a fee when buying bitcoin on an exchange.

When you want to sell your bitcoin or withdraw it (put that money into your bank account for example) there will also be a fee. Additionally, fees apply when you want to send an amount of bitcoin from one user address to another. However, there are exceptions. Some cryptocurrency exchanges offer zero fees for sending bitcoin to other users.

Now that you understand a few basic options for buying bitcoin (along with knowing that there are fees involved) the next question that comes to mind is:

"How Do I Keep My Bitcoin Safe?"

Safety and security are some of the most important questions to consider when getting involved with cryptocurrency. Cryptocurrency is entirely digital; therefore, these digital assets are prone to hacks when stored online.

Holding, or storing, bitcoin online via a cryptocurrency exchange is common and relatively easy for beginners. A cryptocurrency wallet connected to the internet via an exchange is known as a "hot wallet."

Crypto users can also store funds offline, or on a "cold wallet." Some examples of cold wallets are hardware wallets like the Ledger Nano S or Trezor.

There are positives and negatives associated with both hot and cold wallets, but in general, most believe offline wallets to be the most secure solution for storing crypto.

Why? Well, some of you might be familiar with the phrase:

"Not your keys, not your bitcoin."

This essentially means if you don't own your crypto key – in other words if your private key is entrusted to a third-party exchange – then you don't have complete control over your BTC.

Although this is the case, hardware wallets require a user to be entirely in charge of their funds. This means keeping track of the hardware device, knowing the private key, and coming up with/remembering a recovery seed phrase, which is a list of about 22 words that is used to recover funds if a wallet is lost or stolen. For beginners, this process can be stressful, but for those with larger amounts of BTC, a hardware wallet is typically considered a more secure option.

While this book focuses on online exchanges for holding and storing crypto, I do think it's important to briefly mention some best practices for beginners interested in using hardware wallets.

Dave Jevans, chief executive officer of CipherTrace and founder of the hardware wallet IronKey, told me during a phone interview that when purchasing a hardware wallet, it's necessary to know who you are buying the device from.

According to Jevans, there are thousands of people selling hardware wallets on places like eBay for lower prices. I've also seen social media influencers host giveaways on Instagram and Twitter for hardware wallets. While these offers are tempting, you don't know if third-party sellers have tampered with these wallets, which is why it's a best practice to buy hardware wallets directly from a manufacturer's website.

Jevans shared that CipherTrace once dealt with a case involving a customer who lost $10 million worth of bitcoin after purchasing a hardware wallet from a security provider at a trade show. "This customer lost his bitcoin in less than a week," said Jevans.

Jevans also mentioned that when setting up a password recovery phrase for a hardware wallet (or for an online exchange), never store that information on a computer or smartphone. The best thing to do is to write the recovery phrase down on a piece of paper and then store that in something like a safety deposit box.

Clearly, with security comes massive responsibility. This is also the case for those that are tech savvy. A New York Times article written by Bitcoin Billionaire author Nathaniel Popper depicts this well.

In the article Popper describes how a German-born computer programmer living in San Francisco lost track of the password to his crypto hardware wallet containing about $220 million in funds. Stefan Thomas, the programmer, stored his crypto on a small hard drive device known as an "IronKey" (this is the same hardware wallet Jevans helped create).

Although IronKey is known for being one of the world's most secure flash drives (it was even funded by the U.S. Department of Homeland Security), a series of built-in protections has made the device extremely inaccessible.

Unfortunately, Thomas lost track of the paper where he wrote down the password for his IronKey wallet. The IronKey wallet allows users to guess their password 10 times before it encrypts the content in it forever.

According to the article, Thomas has tried eight of his most commonly used password combinations, but none have unlocked the wallet. Only two guesses remain before Thomas's $220 million is lost forever. Yet some bit of hope remains, as we will revisit this topic and possible solutions in Part III.

There are also security concerns with holding crypto on exchanges. To put this into perspective, the well-known cryptocurrency investor Michael Terpin filed a lawsuit against telecommunication giant AT&T in August 2018 for the theft of $24 million worth of cryptocurrency due to SIM swapping.

SIM swapping occurs when a hacker contacts your wireless carrier, convincing the carrier that they are you by disclosing personal data that has been exposed in breaches or through social media. These hackers ultimately try to convince a cellular carrier to switch the SIM card linked to a certain phone number and replace it with a SIM card in their possession. If successful, the hacker will gain access to your incoming and outgoing calls and text messages.

According to Terpin, the SIM swap he experienced was quite unusual. Terpin told me during a phone interview that the attack was caused by a sophisticated criminal gang specifically targeting him. He contends that the gang bribed an AT&T retail store employee, which was followed by a very sophisticated hack of altcoins, or alternative cryptocurrencies, in native wallets.

"This would never happen to a newbie. Most SIM swap losses for newbies are of bitcoin in exchanges where people didn't properly put in their Google Authenticator. I had all of my exchanges and hardware wallets perfectly secured and had no losses of bitcoin or Ethereum or any losses from any exchange whatsoever. So, I'm not your typical victim," said Terpin.

It was later alleged that a 15-year-old hacker was responsible for stealing the $24 million worth of cryptocurrency from Terpin. The hackers attacked and stole from native wallets (cryptocurrencies whose private keys cannot be protected by Google Authenticator and cannot be stored on Ledger or Trezor) relatively unknown tokens whose value had exploded during the initial coin offering boom that year.

Unfortunately, horror stories like this are becoming more common, especially as cryptocurrency enters the mainstream. Although extreme, this is just one example of why users and holders must always consider best practices when it comes to the safety and security of their digital assets.

This is especially critical for users that plan to hold, or "hodl" their bitcoin. The term "hodl" is derived from a misspelling of "hold" in reference to buying and holding bitcoin and other cryptocurrencies. "Hodl" has since become a popular term amongst the cryptocurrency community and is referenced often.

While this might sound daunting – and even turn most people away from wanting to own bitcoin.

Finally, one last important question I've been asked lately is:

"Why Do I Need to Include My Personal Data When Signing Up for A Cryptocurrency Exchange?"

Let's face it, nobody enjoys sharing their personal data. And after hearing about scandals involving Facebook, Google and other tech giants, more people are becoming wary of providing sensitive data over the internet.

This is understandable, but crypto users must be aware that licensed and registered cryptocurrency exchanges operating in the U.S. have anti-money laundering, or AML, programs in place. Oftentimes this means that there is a customer acceptance policy, a customer identification program and ongoing monitoring of transactions and risk management procedures in place.31

In addition to AML procedures, many of these exchanges have known your customer, or KYC processes. Just like a bank requires personal information from users to set up an account, so do most cryptocurrency exchanges today. As such, crypto exchanges may ask users to submit a photo of their driver's license or another document proving their identity.

Simply put, AML and KYC procedures are best practices to ensure that crypto funds are properly used and that users are legitimate. Lana Schwartzman, chief compliance officer of Paxful, a leading cryptocurrency exchange, told me during a phone interview that KYC and AML are very important for any financial business, including cryptocurrency exchanges and marketplaces.

"KYC and AML mean that a crypto exchange is doing what they can to protect customers and their funds. It is the fundamental building block in having controls in place to deter bad actors," she said.

While this is understandable, KYC and AML measures appear to be getting stricter as cryptocurrency gains traction. For example, the Financial Crime Enforcement Network, or FinCEN – which is a unit of the U.S. Treasury Department – is currently pushing for crypto exchanges to collect more data from users transferring over $3,000 in cryptocurrencies into unhosted wallets.

What does this mean exactly?

Say that you have $5,000 worth of BTC stored on a centralized cryptocurrency exchange and you would like to move those funds into a unhosted wallet, like a hardware wallet. If the FinCEN rules that were proposed in December 2020 pass into legislation, crypto exchanges would be required to collect information like the names and home addresses for the owners of unhosted crypto wallets receiving more than $3,000 in cryptocurrencies. If a wallet receives more than $10,000 in aggregate per day, an exchange would be required to file a Currency Transaction Report, or CTR, with FinCEN.

Many in the cryptocurrency community fear that a rule such as this will drive innovation outside of the U.S. since it threatens the digital privacy rights of individuals.

METHODS OF STORING BITCOIN

Bitcoin wallets are going to be similar to bank accounts because this will be where you store, receive, and send out Bitcoins. Keep in mind that just like your bank account, you are going to want to make sure that your wallet is secure so that no one is able to take away your coins!

There are several kinds of wallets that you are going to be able to pick from when it comes to Bitcoin. Software wallets, web wallets and various other ones. There are going to be pros and cons to each wallet, and you are going to be required to make sure that you are doing your research to discover the wallet that is going to be the best for you and what you are going to be doing with Bitcoins. It does not matter what wallet you choose; you will have to make sure that you keep your wallet secure as we just mentioned – and are going to continue to mention because this is extremely important!

Software Wallet

Look at all of your options. Software wallets are one of the original Bitcoin wallets that were created. You will have all kinds of options to pick from when you are looking at using a software wallet. But make sure that you are picking one that is going to allow you to be in complete control of the security of your Bitcoin because of how the software is set up. But you are going to come across a huge hassle that is going to make it to where you have to install the software while making sure to maintain it properly.

Being that blockchain is a public database, any negotiation that moves through the server is not going to be stored but will be verified as well.

The Bitcoin core wallet is the original Bitcoin wallet and has evolved as Bitcoin has evolved. There are a lot of people that are going to say good things about the Bitcoin core wallet while others are going to say dreadful things, but this is how it goes with everything that you are going to use. Going with the original wallet is sometimes going to be the best way for you to go. In order to download this wallet, you are going to need to go to www.Bitcoin.org and download the wallet application. Once the software has been installed on your computer, the portfolio's client is going to attempt to establish a network that way that it can begin to download the blockchain to the appliance.

You will be required to have all of the blocks in the chain before you are going to be able to complete any negotiations with Bitcoin.

There are some other wallets that you can download if you do not want to use Bitcoin core. Every wallet is going to have good points and bad ones that are going to determine how the wallet functions not only on your computer but how it is going to interact with the blockchain. For example, there are going to be some wallets that are going to only be available on Mac computers and it is going to have an app in the app store that will allow you to tie it to the wallet so that you can have access to your wallet and other Bitcoin services on your phone as well as your computer. The armory wallet is a wallet that is going to focus on security over other functions that other wallets may have.

Each wallet will also have its own installation quirk.

The hive wallet will be a wallet that is going to be geared towards beginners. Therefore, you may want to start with this wallet and move on to a different wallet once you have gotten the hang of using Bitcoin.

A lightweight wallet is not going to take up much space on your computer's hard drive as most other wallets will. These thin wallets are going to work faster since they will not be required to download the entire blockchain. If you want to use a lightweight wallet, you may want to consider using Electrum or MultiBit.

You need to think about the fact that thin wallets are not going to be as secure as the wallets that are going to download the entire blockchain. So, if you do not want to lose losing your Bitcoins, you may want to stay away from a lightweight wallet unless you do not have enough room on your hard drive and this is the only way that you can get a portfolio for your Bitcoin.

Web Wallet

You have to make sure that you understand how web wallets work before you decide that this is how you are going to want to store your Bitcoins. A web wallet is going to take a private key that is tied to your wallet and place it on a server that will be controlled by an admin group. There are going to be some web wallets that are going to allow you to link your mobile and software wallets together so that they are all in one place. This wallet is going to make it to where you can access it anywhere at any time as long as you have internet access, this is why web wallets are so popular. The website is going to be in charge of your public and private key which makes it to where Bitcoins can be taken without you knowing about it.

There are a lot of web wallets that have security breaches; which is why you are going to need to research your wallet before you decide that you want to use it or else you are going to end up losing some of your coins without having the chance to get them back.

Whenever you pick out your web wallet, there are going to be a lot that say that they are focusing on keeping tight security for their consumers so that they can pull customers in. Some wallets you are going to want to bear in mind are Circle, Coinbase, and Xapo.

Coinbase will allow you to use it worldwide as well as giving you offers that you are only going to be able to use with Coinbase. They are also going to provide a trade service between the United States and Europe.

Xapo will be a simple wallet that is consumer friendly and going to offer some extra security that is known as a cold storage vault.

The circle will allow the citizens of the United States to link their bank accounts to their web wallets that way they can deposit money. When it comes to the consumers in other countries, they are only going to be able to use debit or credit cards.

You may want to consider using a wallet that is anonymous. The world of Bitcoin is going to make it to where you can stay completely anonymous which means that no one is going to know who you are. There are going to be some web wallets that are going to offer less security and are not going to offer you any insurance. A dark wallet is going to be an extension of chrome, and it is one of the most popular anonymous wallets. The servers are going to fluctuate to offer the stability that you need for your Bitcoins. But the server is going to be vulnerable and is going to be open to being hacked at any time.

There are going to be a few anonymous wallets that are going to contain features that will offer faster cash outs than other wallets will.

Hardware Wallet

You have to consider hardware wallets when you are looking at a portfolio to use for Bitcoin. If you are overly protective of your finances and your money, then you will want to go with a hardware wallet. A hardware wallet is going to be a physical device that is going to hold a private key and work electronically as well as be able to facilitate payments like any other wallet would be able to do. These wallets are going to be able to be carried on your person and will not require you to rely on a third party for storing your Bitcoins.

A hardware wallet is going to be immune to any type of virus such as a Trojan virus that is going to steal your login credentials and credit card or online banking account details.

When you buy a hardware wallet, there are going to be a lot of different wallets that you are going to be able to choose from. They are going to range in quality as well as price range.

A Pi wallet will use a cold storage method and is not going to have a wireless capability that you could be searching for. It is going to use the Armory client that the Armory wallet uses so that it is secure enough for you to work with without requiring you to set up your own wallet. It is going to be consumer friendly as well as be safe for you to use as a hardware wallet.

A USB wallet is going to be affordable and is getting to be more popular as a portfolio choice for those that use with Bitcoins. These devices will help to protect the data that you place on them and will contain a microprocessor chip that is going to be similar to the chip that a credit card is going to use. USB wallets are going to allow you to use it with different computers so that the device is connected through a secure connection.

Trezor is going to be similar to the Pi wallet, but it is going to have a small screen that you are going to use for interaction. There are going to be some private keys that you are going to be using because they are generated by the device. The Trezor is going to be immune to malware attacks.

Ensure that you are encrypting the wallet that you are using. There are a lot of hardware wallets that are going to require that you put a code or password in which will cause it to become encrypted whenever it is initialized. If your device does not require you to create a password for it, then you are going to want to think about it due to the fact that it is going to make your wallet more secure. Each hardware wallet will require a different protocol that you will have to follow so that you are establishing a secure encrypted connection.

CONCLUSION

Bitcoin is as of now the most important and generally received computerized money. A developing number of organizations, charities and different associations are now accepting bitcoin payments going from e-retailers to law offices to sports establishments. Further, late inflationary and banking emergencies across the globe have featured a portion of the key dangers intrinsic to fiat money. This sets out extra open doors for decentralized digital currencies. Quality education is key to expanding Bitcoin's acceptance and utilization by merchants, establishments and people. The system will likewise have to address criticisms around illegal utilization of bitcoin and work determinedly to fabricate administrative and lawful systems around the globe.

The buying and selling of cryptocurrencies are currently seen as something totally speculative, although increasingly real for daily use thanks to the cards offered by many of these websites and apps.

The names of cryptocurrencies have acronyms and as one thing is the name of the currency and another is the name of the platform that created the cryptocurrency, sometimes the terms are often confused.

For example, the cryptocurrency Stellar is actually the name of the platform and the cryptocurrency is called Lumens (XLM).

Be careful with using unreliable websites or trusting people who guarantee you easy and fast income. Basically, you have to be as careful as with anything else.

In the future I am convinced that we will be surprised by the day when we used real coins and bills.

In your bank, physical money does not exist. They are virtual data that the bank has.

I recommend buying cryptocurrencies that have a low value such as Stellar and / or Ripple and that are also backed by a large company.

Stellar, for example, is supported by IBM or Ripple, which has more than 100 allies.

The increase in value or the loss of most cryptocurrencies are closely linked to Bitcoin, that is, if Bitcoin goes up, the rest go up, if Bitcoin goes down, the rest go down.

Something very important is to always have your passwords to access your virtual wallets stored in a safe place like a safe, since in case of losing the password there is no way to recover your virtual money.

On the other hand, something cumbersome is the registration in these websites and apps since being a financial process they behave with the regulation of any bank and therefore they will ask you for a lot of information such as your photo of an identification card (DNI, passport or card driving, etc.), telephone, email, address...

Remember that from my point of view you should invest in Bitcoins and other cryptocurrencies only money that you will never need since there is a lot of volatility in the market.

As we end this book, I would like you to remember that Bitcoin is a technology and the blockchain is a technology, that Bitcoin will not be the only cryptocurrency, but that cryptocurrency will be part of our daily lives.

Thank you for reading this book. I hope you found it useful and that you have learned something new.

www.ingramcontent.com/pod-product-compliance
Lightning Source LLC
Chambersburg PA
CBHW071520210326
41597CB00018B/2820